SYMBOLS OF AMERICAN FREEDOM

The Lincoln Memorial

by Kirsten Chang

BLASTOFF! READERS

BELLWETHER MEDIA • MINNEAPOLIS, MN

Note to Librarians, Teachers, and Parents:

Blastoff! Readers are carefully developed by literacy experts and combine standards-based content with developmentally appropriate text.

Level 1 provides the most support through repetition of high-frequency words, light text, predictable sentence patterns, and strong visual support.

Level 2 offers early readers a bit more challenge through varied simple sentences, increased text load, and less repetition of high-frequency words.

Level 3 advances early-fluent readers toward fluency through increased text and concept load, less reliance on visuals, longer sentences, and more literary language.

Level 4 builds reading stamina by providing more text per page, increased use of punctuation, greater variation in sentence patterns, and increasingly challenging vocabulary.

Level 5 encourages children to move from "learning to read" to "reading to learn" by providing even more text, varied writing styles, and less familiar topics.

Whichever book is right for your reader, Blastoff! Readers are the perfect books to build confidence and encourage a love of reading that will last a lifetime!

This edition first published in 2019 by Bellwether Media, Inc.

No part of this publication may be reproduced in whole or in part without written permission of the publisher. For information regarding permission, write to Bellwether Media, Inc., Attention: Permissions Department, 6012 Blue Circle Drive, Minnetonka, MN 55343.

Library of Congress Cataloging-in-Publication Data

Names: Chang, Kirsten, 1991- author.
Title: The Lincoln Memorial / by Kirsten Chang.
Description: Minneapolis, MN : Bellwether Media, Inc., 2019. | Series: Blastoff! Readers: Symbols of American Freedom | Includes bibliographical references and index.
Identifiers: LCCN 2018030411 (print) | LCCN 2018031098 (ebook) | ISBN 9781681036472 (ebook) | ISBN 9781626179165 (hardcover : alk. paper) | ISBN 9781618914934 (pbk. : alk. paper)
Subjects: LCSH: Lincoln Memorial (Washington, D.C.)–Juvenile literature. | Lincoln, Abraham, 1809-1865–Monuments–Washington (D.C.)–Juvenile literature. | Washington (D.C.)–Buildings, structures, etc.–Juvenile literature.
Classification: LCC F203.4.L73 (ebook) | LCC F203.4.L73 C47 2019 (print) | DDC 975.3–dc23
LC record available at https://lccn.loc.gov/2018030411

Editor: Rebecca Sabelko   Designer: Andrea Schneider

Printed in the United States of America, North Mankato, MN.

Table of Contents

What Is the Lincoln Memorial?	4
A Nation at War	8
Free People	18
Glossary	22
To Learn More	23
Index	24

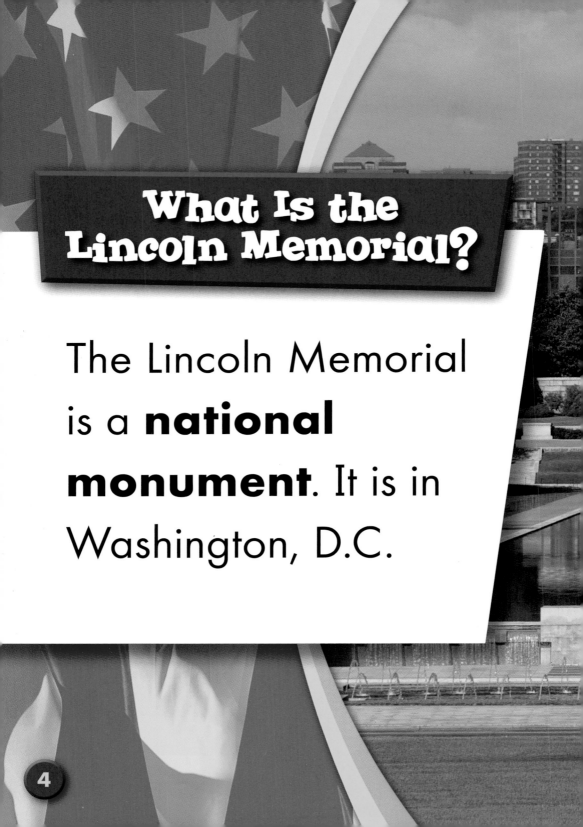

What Is the Lincoln Memorial?

The Lincoln Memorial is a **national monument**. It is in Washington, D.C.

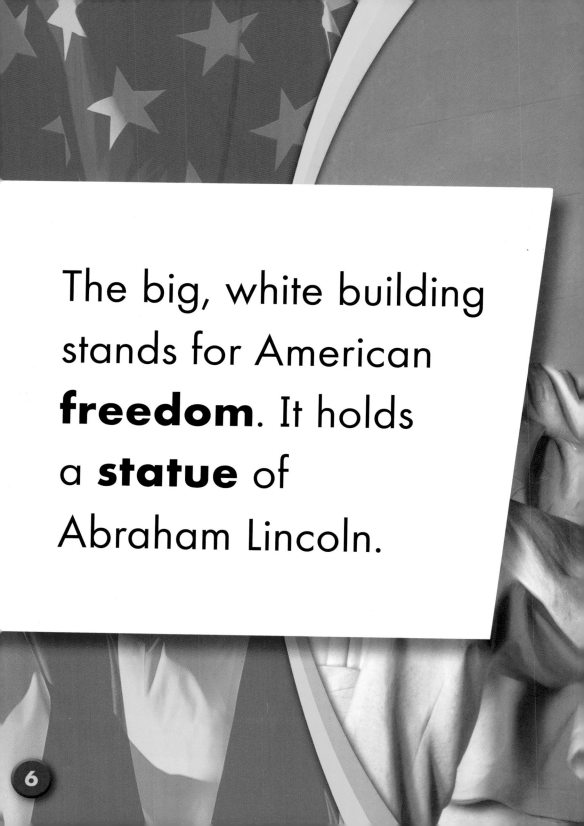

The big, white building stands for American **freedom**. It holds a **statue** of Abraham Lincoln.

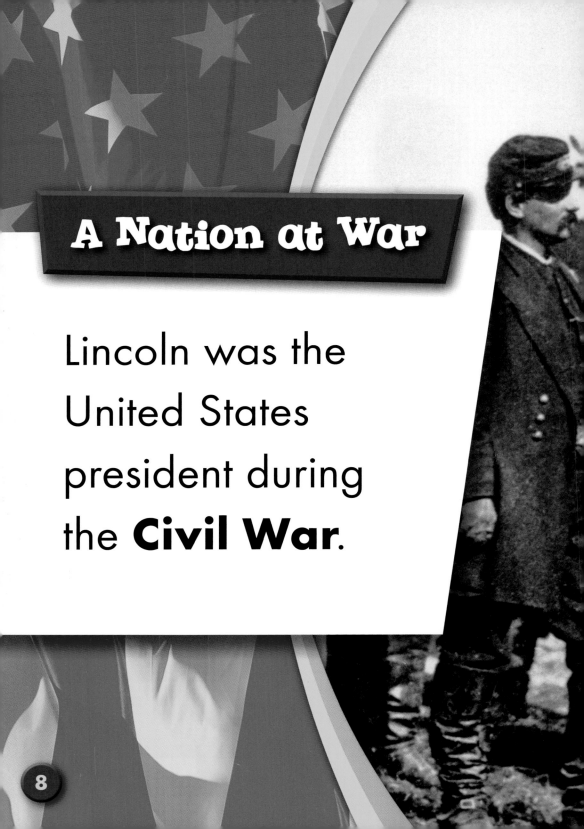

A Nation at War

Lincoln was the United States president during the **Civil War**.

8

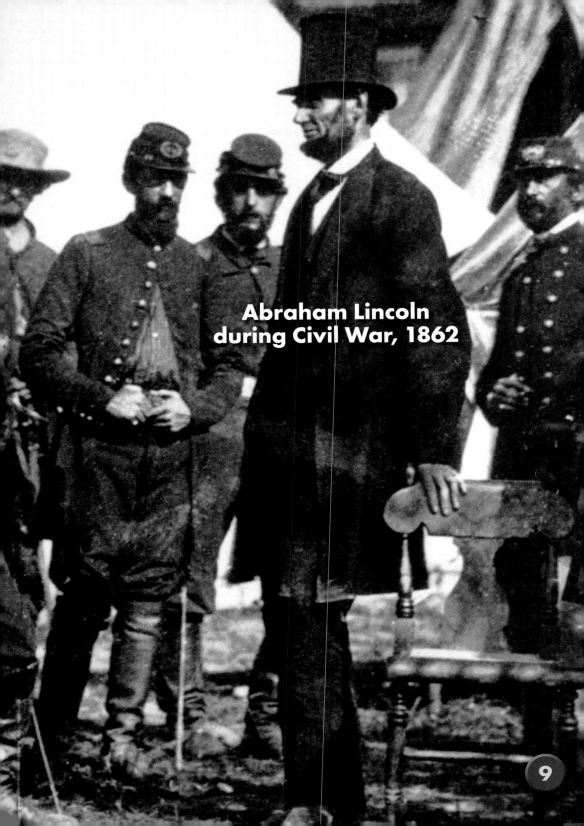

Abraham Lincoln
during Civil War, 1862

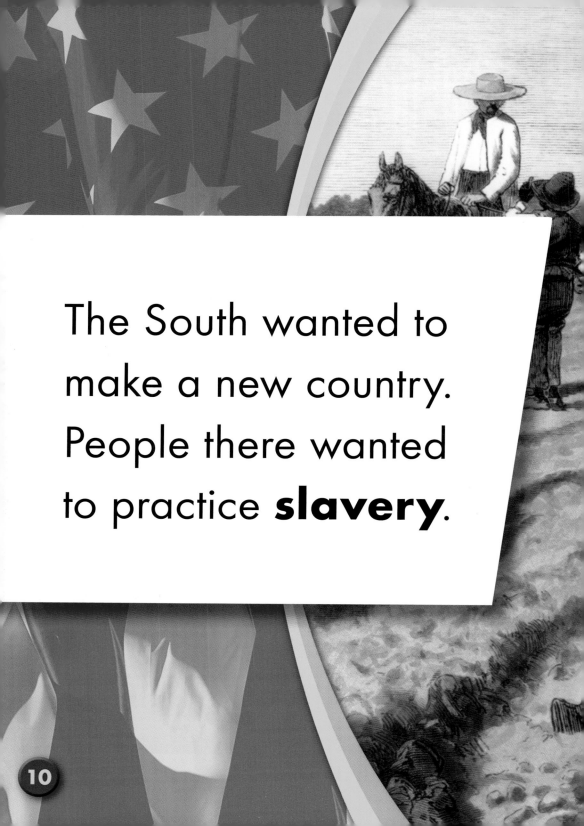

The South wanted to make a new country. People there wanted to practice **slavery**.

slaves working in field
during the 1860s

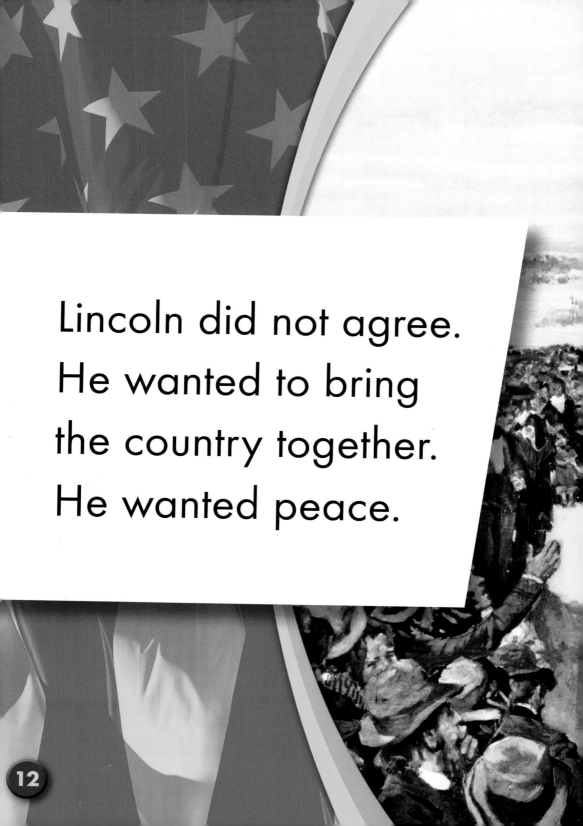

Lincoln did not agree. He wanted to bring the country together. He wanted peace.

Lincoln giving Gettysburg Address

He soon signed
a new **law**.
It freed the slaves!

1861
Abraham
Lincoln
becomes
president and
the Civil War
begins

1865
Civil War
ends

1863
Slaves
are freed

1922
Lincoln
Memorial
opens

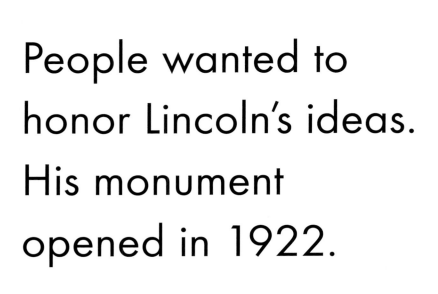

People wanted to
honor Lincoln's ideas.
His monument
opened in 1922.

Free People

People visit the monument to celebrate freedom.

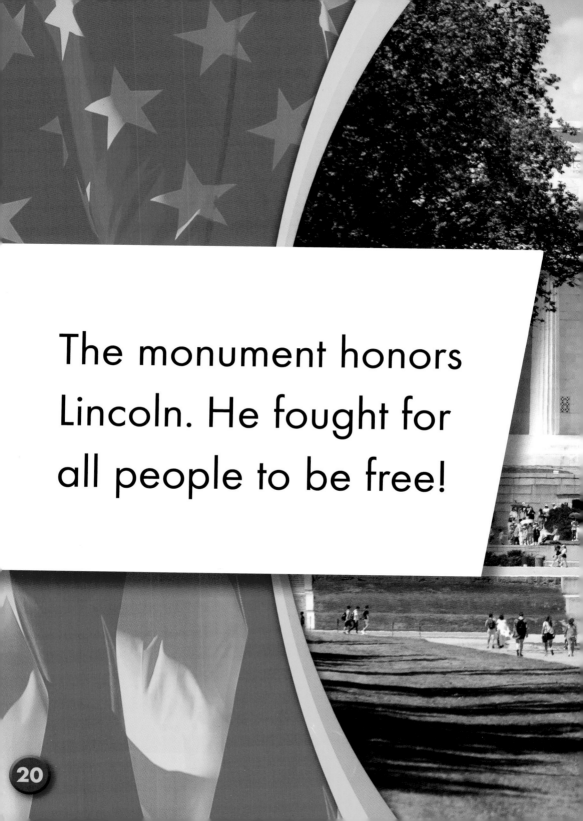

The monument honors Lincoln. He fought for all people to be free!

Glossary

Civil War

the U.S. war between the northern states and the southern states

national monument

a statue or building that is important to the country

freedom

the state of being free

slavery

the practice of owning people who work for no money

law

a rule made by the government that must be followed

statue

an image of a person made out of a solid material such as stone

To Learn More

AT THE LIBRARY

Duling, Kaitlyn. *Lincoln Memorial*.
Minneapolis, Minn.: Bullfrog Books, 2018.

Kissock, Heather. *Lincoln Memorial*. New
York, N.Y.: Smartbook Media Inc., 2017.

Murray, Julie. *Lincoln Memorial*. Minneapolis,
Minn.: Abdo Kids, 2017.

ON THE WEB

FACTSURFER

Factsurfer.com gives you
a safe, fun way to find
more information.

1. Go to www.factsurfer.com.

2. Enter "Lincoln Memorial" into the
   search box.

3. Click the "Surf" button and select your
   book cover to see a list of related web sites.

Index

Civil War, 8, 9, 15

freedom, 6, 14, 15, 18, 20

law, 14

Lincoln, Abraham, 6, 8, 9, 12, 13, 15, 16, 20

national monument, 4, 16, 18, 20

peace, 12

president, 8, 15

slavery, 10, 11, 14, 15

South, 10

statue, 6

timeline, 15

United States, 8

Washington, D.C., 4